The Big Day!
A New Baby Arrives

Nicola Barber

First published in 2008 by Wayland

This paperback edition published in 2011 by Wayland

Copyright © Wayland 2008

Wayland
338 Euston Road
London NW1 3BH

Wayland Australia
Level 17/207 Kent Street
Sydney, NSW 2000

Editor: Camilla Lloyd
Designer: Elaine Wilkinson
Picture Researcher: Kathy Lockley

Picture Acknowledgments: The author and publisher would like to thank the following for their pictures to be reproduced in this publication: Cover photograph: Larry Williams/zefa/Corbis; Chuck Savage/Corbis: 17; CuboImages srl/Alamy Images: 19; David Oliver/Stone/Getty Images: 1, 11; Jenny Acheson/Riser/Getty Images: 13; John James/Alamy Images: 10, 24; Jose Luis Pelaez, Inc/Corbis: 15; Larry Williams/zefa/Corbis: 16; Michael Keller/Corbis: 12; Owen Franken/Corbis: 14, 21; Patrick Lacroix/The Image Bank/Getty Images: 9; Phillipe Lissac/Godong/Corbis: 18; Ross Whitaker/The Image Bank/Getty Images: 20; Sally & Richard Greenhill/Alamy Images: 6; Stewart Cohen/Blend Images/Getty Images: 7; Superstudio/Iconica/Getty Images: 5; Tim Brown/Stone/Getty Images: 8.

British Library Cataloguing in Publication Data:
Barber, Nicola
  New baby. - (The big day)
  1. Brothers and sisters - Juvenile literature 2. Newborn
  infants - Care - Juvenile literature
  I. Title
  306.8'75

ISBN: 978 0 7502 6517 1

Printed in China

Wayland is a division of Hachette Children's Books, an Hachette UK company

www.hachette.co.uk

Contents

Mum is having a baby

Your Mum is having a baby. The baby has been growing inside your Mum for nearly nine months.

What will the new baby be like?

Now Mum's tummy is big, and sometimes you can feel the baby moving around inside. Soon it will be time for the baby to be born.

Getting ready

It's fun to help your Mum and Dad get everything ready for the new baby.

You can help to choose the decorations for the baby's room.

You can buy some toys for the new baby
to play with.

Meeting the baby

When it's time for the baby to be born, your Mum will probably go to the hospital.

Soon you can go to meet your new brother or sister. What is it like holding the baby for the first time?

Welcoming the baby

Sometimes, if a baby is born early, he or she may stay in hospital for a little while.

Your Mum will help to look after the baby in the hospital.

Usually your Mum and the baby will come home after a few days. It's fun to have a new brother or sister at home. But babies can make a lot of noise!

Sharing

It probably feels different at home with the new baby. Mum and Dad are often busy. But you can still have special family times together.

While Dad looks after the baby, Mum might take you to the library, or for a bike ride.

Helping with the baby

You can help Mum and Dad to look after the baby. You might be able to feed the baby, or change the baby's nappy.

You can enjoy the peace and quiet when the baby is asleep!

Bathtime

Bathtime is fun with the new baby.
The baby has a special small bath.

You can help to wash the baby,
and play with the bath toys.

After a bath,
it is often time for
the baby to go to sleep.

Naming the baby

Your family might have a special ceremony to welcome the new baby.

This baby is being named in a Hindu ceremony, twelve days after her birth.

This baby is having water poured over her head at her baptism. This is a Christian ceremony when the baby is named and welcomed into the Christian religion.

First birthday

Babies grow up and change very quickly. Soon your baby brother or sister will be sitting up and crawling around.

You will always remember the day
when your brother or sister was born —
because this is their birthday.

Happy first birthday!

Baby words

If you are writing about your new baby brother or sister, these are some of the words you might need to use.

Baptism

Feed

Bathtime

Hospital

Birthday

Nappy

Brother

Sister

Ceremony

Sleep

Crawling

Toy

Further information

Books

I'm a Big Brother by Joanna Cole, Eos, 1997

I'm a Big Sister by Joanna Cole, Eos, 2000

The New Baby (Topsy and Tim Storybooks) by Jean and Gareth Adamson, Ladybird Books, 2003

The New Baby at Your House by Joanna Cole, William Morrow, 1999

There's a House Inside My Mummy by Giles Andreae, Orchard Books, 2002

Welcoming a New Baby (My Family and Me) by Mary Auld, Franklin Watts, 2007

Website for children

http://www.kidshealth.org/kid/feeling/home_family/new_baby.html

Websites for parents

http://www.kidshealth.org/parent/emotions/feelings/sibling_prep.html

http://www.parentlineplus.org.uk/index.php?id=684

http://www.understandingchildhood.net/leaflets.html

Index

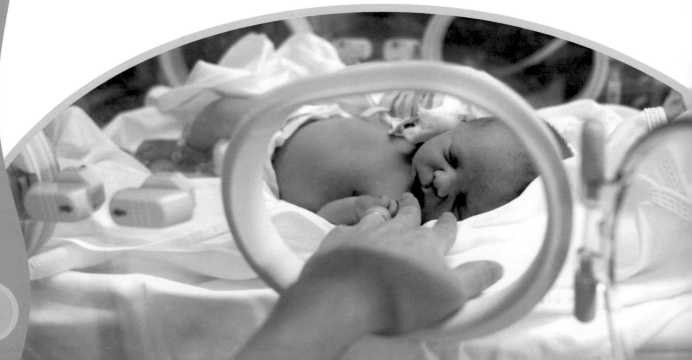